John Bradshaw and Harry Moss at work
in the Cotton Exchange in 1967

CLOCKING ON...

PLESSEY, Ford, Littlewoods, Courtaulds, Higson's, Pendleton's, Dunlop, Tate & Lyle – what do those names mean to you...?

If they bring a warm glow of nostalgia for a lost era, then you are not alone. For in many a Liverpool home lives a former worker who will remember with pride and passion the great names that employed thousands and thousands of Merseysiders.

These firms were the backdrop to the working life of communities the length and breadth of Merseyside, at a time when factories employed generation after generation and when life often revolved around the job. Work was not just 9 to 5, it was a part of life.

The Way We Worked II shows their resilience, their pride in their work but above all their comradeship and spirit. So many memories, so many smiles.

SPREAD THE WORD

Lever Brothers margarine factory at Port Sunlight, June 1932

JOBS FOR LIFE

Above, unloading the van at The Distillers Company, Speke, 1947. Left, Harold Wilson talks with workers at the stock yard of Unit Construction as he opens a factory at Kirkby, Liverpool, in 1964. Below, the ladies at Dista Products in Speke

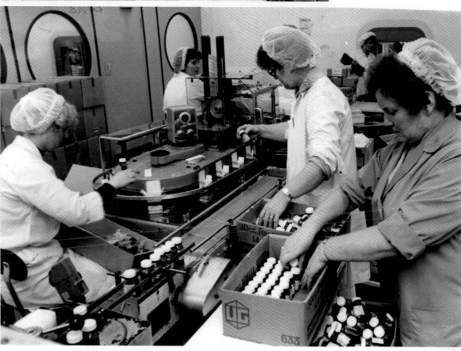

Pupils at fitting benches at the Preparatory Training Centre, Rathbone Road, Liverpool, expanded for use as a full government training centre for instruction in engineering trades, at Liverpool Labour Exchange, July 1940

On the assembly line at Elexcel
Electric Company, Liverpool, fitting
together an aeroplane control panel

Hot off the press – Linotype
machines pump out the news at
the Liverpool Daily Post & Echo

Save our jobs – a protest against the closure of the Meccano factory in 1979

DRIVING FORCE

Workers leaving the Halewood Ford factory in 1971 – the Ford Halewood plant officially opened on Friday, March 8, 1963. Ford certainly captured the imagination of Liverpool and there have been many highs, and lows, during Halewood's rollercoaster journey...

WHEN THE CHIPS ARE DOWN

Lovely! That's 20 years old Margaret Barber's verdict on the mass-production chips she is eating in 1967. Margaret was one of the chip-loving workers at the giant Ford Car factory at Halewood. Below, women workers from the Ford Plant in Halewood wait to enter the headquarters of the Transport and General Workers Union for a mass meeting in June 1968

Hard at work in the car factory in 1967, where staff experienced continuous noise levels of 90 to 100 decibels

The 20,000th Merseyside car – an Escort –
on its way to Finland in 1968, hoisted aboard
the 1,374-ton motor vessel Helics at Garston
Docks. The car was one of a shipment of 250
for Helsinki. Large export orders meant a big
increase in traffic at both Liverpool and Garston
Docks, and in an attempt to effect a smooth
flow of cars, Ford and the shipping companies
pioneered the use of drive-on drive-off ships

STARTER'S ORDERS

Top left, striking workers at Ford's Halewood factory make a vote with their hands during a meeting in April 1971. Left, heading through the factory gates on a March morning in 1969. Above, the design of a Ford Anglia engine is inspected in 1964

Production of the new Capri at the Ford Halewood plant in 1975 – despite the difficulties and shortages of the three-day week, output of the Capri II ran at 200-300 a day.

PEOPLE POWER

12,000 workers at Ford's body and assembly plant at Halewood voted to accept the company's pay deal in 1977. The meeting took place at South Liverpool FC's ground. Below, we like the flares boys! A thumbs-up from happy Ford workers after the end of a dispute in 1978

Workers leave Halewood in 1976

ESCORT GHIA

A motoring milestone – the 4-millionth Escort to be produced in Europe is driven off the production line at the Merseyside factory in 1997

MOTOR CITY

Vauxhall Vivas destined for the Canadian market being loaded aboard the SS La Primavera at Ellesmere Port in 1968. The ship, on charter to Vauxhall Motors, carried 850 cars each month

The busy production line at Vauxhall Motors, Ellesmere Port, in 1965. Below, Viva bodies are washed down and sanded, prior to their first coat of paint, in the largest 'wet deck' in Europe in 1969

GOOD TIMES, BAD TIMES
John Turnbull and Dave Hurley share a joke with Frank McCoy of the shop stewards committee in 1979

LIFE IN THE FAST LANE
Assembly of differential gears, crown-wheel and pinion is a high precision operation

VAUX POPS
28 new starters clock on at Vauxhall Motors in 1986. It brought the number of new jobs created there to 1,000 in just 18 months. The jobs boom was thanks to the introduction of the new Astra and marked a turnaround in the fortune of the company from the black days of January, 1981, when the company axed a third of the workforce

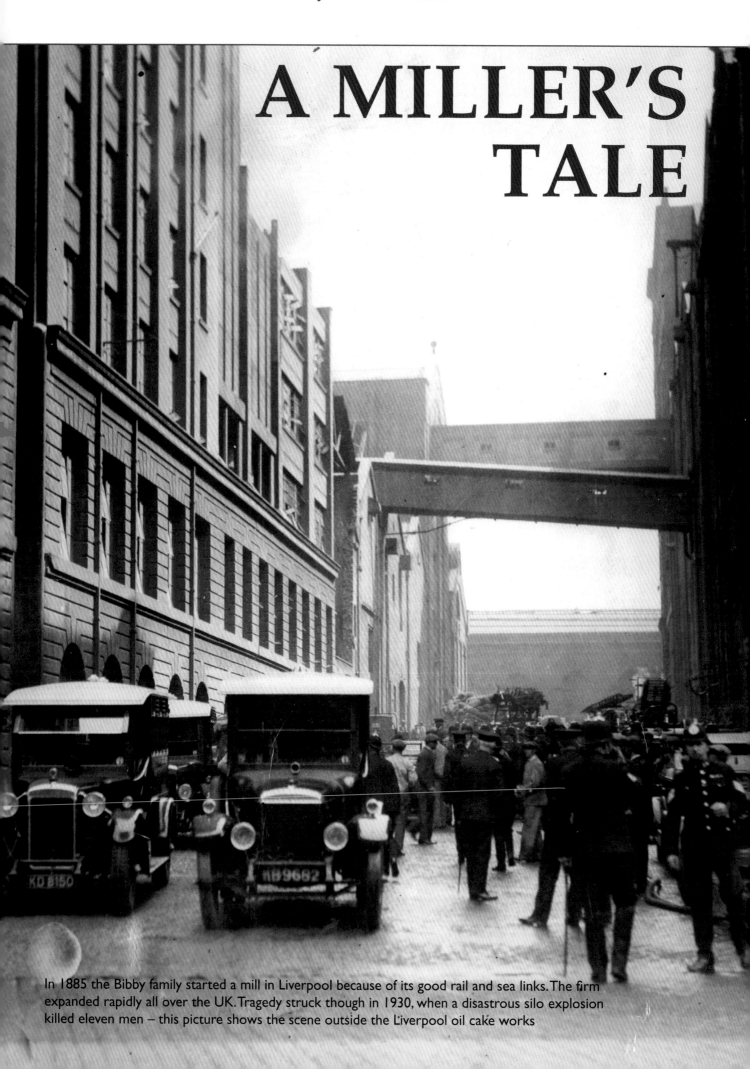

A MILLER'S TALE

In 1885 the Bibby family started a mill in Liverpool because of its good rail and sea links. The firm expanded rapidly all over the UK. Tragedy struck though in 1930, when a disastrous silo explosion killed eleven men – this picture shows the scene outside the Liverpool oil cake works

HAT'S OFF
Princess Margaret's visit to Bibby's in 1982

PUSH THE BUTTON

Above, hi-tech training for John Foxtrot at Bibby's edible oils plant in Bootle in 1986. John had a typical foreman's job at the old plant – supervising 13 men in the oilseed crushing department, monitoring progress against production targets, correcting faults and coordinating maintenance. In his new job, the processes were the same, but the equipment little short of revolutionary

END OF AN ERA

Peter Hardman remembers the huge Bibby's factory in its heyday, when as a lad he made regular visits to pick up cattle feed for his father's farm in Bolton. But in 1988 the demolition expert was in charge of breaking up the Great Howard Street site and watching the last brick hit the ground. A few of the buildings dated back to the late 1800s with most built in the 1930s. At its peak, around the second world war, about 5,000 people worked there. Production at the seed crushing and vegetable oil refinery finally ceased in June 1987

Dried beans being unloaded in 1942

DOCKING IN

Ship's log – the new weighbridge at Toxteth Dock in 1949, handling West African timber imported by Elder Dempster Line vessels

The town with a shipyard on its mind – workers at Cammell Laird in Birkenhead, ponder their future in May, 1970

Unloading goods at
Liverpool's docks in 1938

A ship's hold full of
milk churns, 1949

TOUGH TALKS

Above, Hugh Gaitskell MP chats
with Liverpool dockers over a mug
of tea in Gladstone Dock canteen,
1958. Below, Jack Jones, member of
the Labour Party's policy-forming
National Executive Committee,
attends a meeting with the dockers
strike committee in 1967.

A precariously balanced
cargo of goods in 1938

Left, Mr Champion, shipping manager of the BICC (Prescot) and Mr Harper, managing director of Harper & Mylrea Ltd haulage contractors, check the state board at the Port Information Centre in the Mersey Docks & Harbour Board building, in 1966

PORT OF CALL

The first day of calls for Liverpool's Port Information Centre, on January 11, 1966, proved to be a very busy one. The first of its kind in the country, the information centre was opened by Mersey Docks & Harbour Board as an aid to maintaining a smooth flow of traffic through the port. Telephone and radio controllers were in contact with a roving patrol in the docks to give the latest information about each of the berths. Above, Carol Harper types out a message, while Mr Flaherty (right) reports from Alexandra Dock

STRETCH OF THE IMAGINATION

The Dunlop Rubber Company employed many thousands of people at its factory in Speke, making everything from tyres and golf balls to footwear. Of course, Dunlop also had a major factory in Rice Lane, Walton

RUBBER SOLE

New balls please! Top left, a painting machine, 1965. The minimum of handling preserves the condition of the ball. Above, the car tyre moulding department. Left, the footwear lines begin the night shift

BOUNCING BACK

Below, Dunlop workers vote on the Six Point Plan in January 1978. Speke wives picket Dunlop's head office in London in 1979, protesting against plans to close the Merseyside factory

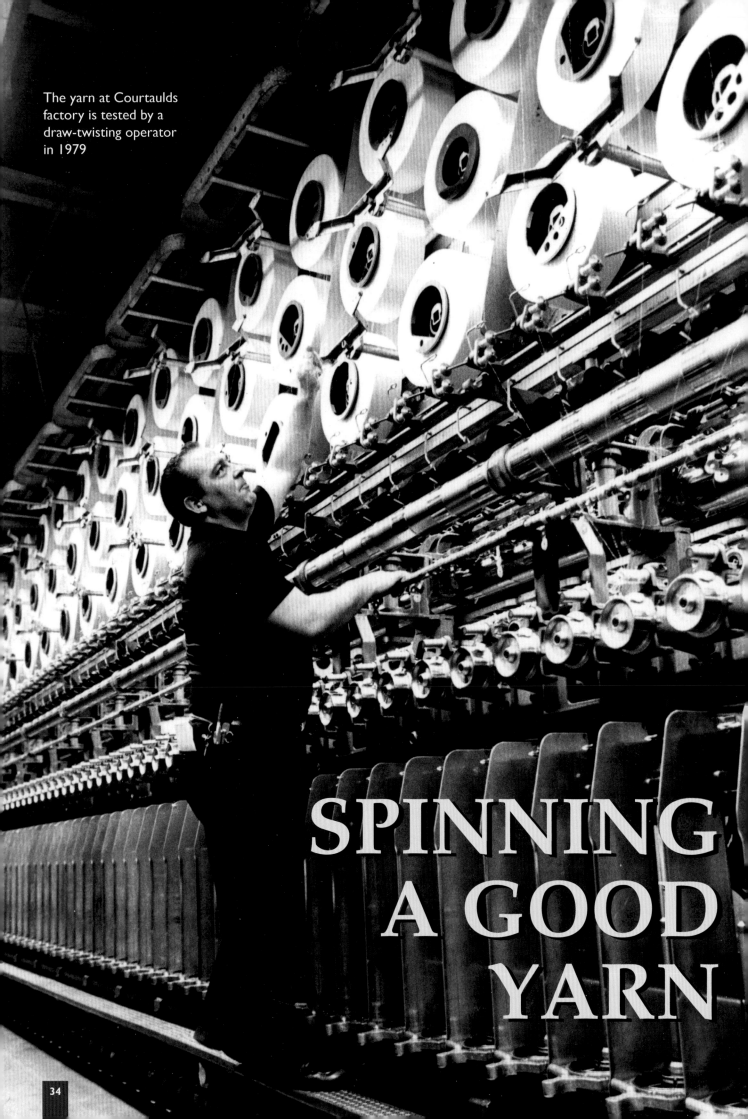

The yarn at Courtaulds factory is tested by a draw-twisting operator in 1979

SPINNING A GOOD YARN

HOW MEN OF FIBRE BUILT AN EMPIRE

Aerial view of the Courtauld's Group Aintree factory in 1966. Originally the British Enka, it produced rayon textile yarn, tyre yarn and cellulose film, later moving into ceylon nylon yarn, warp knitting, dyeing and paint manufacture

Two men with more than 60 years of service at Courtaulds between them – Frank Hughes and Tommy Bamford

An informal meeting on the steps of Courtaulds in 1976

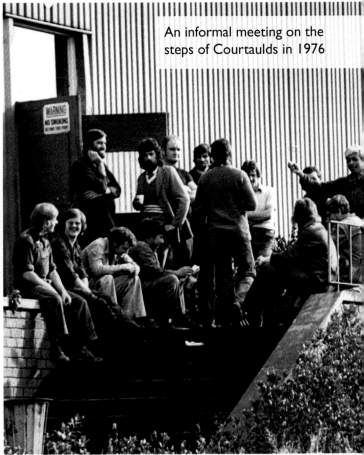

RAISE THE WOOF

Actress Gilly Coman (who played Avaline in Bread) with some of the Courtaulds workers who raised over £800 for the Guide Dogs for the Blind charity in 1989. This was the second time they had raised enough money to train a dog. The latest recruit was called 'Mongy'

Skelmersdale workers travel to London to protest against the company's plans to close their weaving mill, 1976

Action committee leaders discuss the day's events in 1981

ELECTRIC DREAMS

The GEC / English Electric
works in Fazakerley in 1978

Parts for water turbines
in Canada and India
in production at the
English Electric factory
in Netherton, 1968

Bright sparks in the factory workshop of English Electric, 1958

Some of the 1,500 English Electric marchers on their way to Liverpool Stadium during a protest in 1969

RINGING THE CHANGES

Edge Lane was the home to the ATM Company, AT&E (Automatic Telephone & Electric), Plessey, GPT and Marconi for over 100 years, whilst these companies were at the hub of the UK Telecommunications industry. John Nicolson recalls his time working at Plessey's . . .

SO many people worked at the Edge Lane site – it was 'life' for thousands of people. At one time, it was second to the Ford Motor Company as the biggest employer in Liverpool and Merseyside.

Yet the ordinary Liverpudlian didn't seem to know exactly what we had produced or who we had sold 'it' to. They didn't realise that, every time they made a telephone call it was extremely likely that they were being connected by equipment that was designed (at least in part), or manufactured or tested at the Edge Lane site.

This equipment had come from under their noses, be it AT&E, Plessey, GPT or Marconi. Made in Edge Lane - the hub of the UK Telecommunications industry.

On September 22, 1975 I started work at Plessey's as a Technician Apprentice. My home in Halewood was about 6 or 7 miles from Edge Lane and it was a number 65 bus journey to work for me. Leaving Halewood at 7:15 a.m. it took 35 minutes to get to Edge Lane on a journey that took in Mackets Lane, Belle Vale, Netherley and Childwall.

The bus was often full before it had reached Belle Vale. As it reached the top of Edge Lane, at the junction with Oswald Street, a small group of people would usually get off, but the vast majority remained on board until the stop outside Plessey.

I started two weeks behind two other Technician Apprentices, John McKnight and Alun Jones, and so I had a bit of catching up to do. Both John's Mum and Dad worked for Plessey as did Alun's brother. As my sister Susan had also worked there I guess there was some sort ➤

➤ of policy which favoured relations of current staff but I wasn't going to complain. There was also about 30 lads on an EITB (Engineering Industry Training Board) course which was effectively being run in parallel with our training for the first 12 months.

This made things a little uncomfortable from time to time as most of the EITB trainees looked upon us, the 'Plessey 3', as 'the haves' and themselves as the 'have-nots'. They had to wear a blue overall whereas we were often exempt from the dress code so that meant an obvious demarcation line was drawn between us and them but that scenario was a familiar part of life at Plessey in the 70s and 80s.

One of the first examples of this that I can remember was the management restaurant. All of the managers wore a shirt and tie and they had access to an exclusive area where, I guess (because I was never to get there in person) they had nicer chairs and tables with clean cutlery and perhaps even some sort of table service.

Downstairs in the workers canteen, it was a different story.

Lesson time at AT&E, circa 1965

Hundreds of people piled in at almost the same time to fill themselves with, certainly in my case, good old 70's style junk food – pie, chips and beans! The hourly paid (mostly production workers) had a 45 minute lunch break whereas we, the staff (of which the apprentices were part of) had a 48-minute lunch. There was approximately 13,000 people employed on the site when I started there. Being such a large organisation meant that the site included shops and facilities such as a company doctor, dentist and a bank.

Earning a wage and now really living in the adult world made you rather 'cocky' and full of oneself and one of the first 'lessons' in coming down to earth came my way from the company doctor.

It was on one of my first days in work and I had been sent for the compulsory medical. I knocked on the door and marched in, not realising that I was chewing gum.

The doctor did realise, screaming at me to 'get out' and 'don't you dare walk into my surgery chewing gum', bursting my eardrums as I beat a hasty retreat out through the door.

In a similar way around the same time I took up enough courage to march into the Dryden pub, which was just outside the Milton Road entrance on Edge Lane, for the first time. Obviously under age (given my youthful looks) I compounded my natural discomfort by asking for a PINT of brown bitter!

"Are you 18?" said the manager.

Home time as workers leave AT&E

"Yeah" I said in a high-pitched voice. But he served me anyway so my initiation was over.

At 4:31pm my working day ended. Heading back to Edge Lane across the wasteland between the covered way and the shops which lined the road, it was quite an amazing site to see a row of buses lined up as far as you could see looking towards the city centre.

These would quickly fill up and head off to the suburbs.

And this was just for the staff. The hourly paid didn't finish until 5 o'clock when the same amount of buses would again fill the inside lane of the dual carriageway until they too moved off, invariably full, to take people home.

When I was an apprentice, the site was still producing the ironwork and mechanical parts for the electromechanical Strowger and Crossbar switching systems. I can still recall the smell of the machine shops. These occupied the area which was later to become the System X unit, Building 3.

Apprentices had to work in most of the departments around the site, so we had a 'licence' to roam into almost any of the buildings.

The machine shops offered a sheltered route between the covered way and the reception and personnel offices over at the Bullnose building. I don't think I will ever forget the noise the machines made as they hammered out pieces of metal nor the smell of the Swarfega and oil. There was a rather sad looking old chap who was usually sat smoking his pipe next to 'his' machine as it hammered away. He was probably in his fifties then and I always felt sorry for him given the noise and conditions he worked in, although I don't think I ever thought about the effect the pipe might be having on his health, as it seemed to be a permanent feature.

Smoking was allowed almost anywhere and everywhere in those days, including it seemed whilst you worked. The first department I worked in was AC9 – in 1976 it was anything but noisy and smelly. It produced printed circuit boards for TXE4 (as the company was now moving into electronic equipment and away from the electro-mechanical Strowger) and I had a brief spell working alongside the Test Engineers, some of whom became such good friends that they still are today. ➤

CONNECTING PEOPLE

Above and below, life at Automatic Telephone & Electric. Left, inside the Plessey workshop

➤ When my apprenticeship was over, I found a temporary position in the training department which had temporarily been relocated to Gillmoss due to the site modernisation programme at Edge Lane. This was perhaps the funniest 18-months of my working life. Computers, in the every day working sense, didn't exist then.

So everything was hand-written and then typed by a small group of typists.

The manager of the section did not like me one little bit. Needless to say he was forever on the look out for me, questioning what I was doing and telling his sub-managers to keep an eye on me and asking them why was I always laughing.

Well, I was always laughing because of the tricks and pranks my colleagues were determined to exercise on a daily basis. The main bulk of the dept sat in four rows of desks, with four desks in each row.

At 18-years-old, I was the youngest in the department, the ages of the rest of the team ranging from early twenties to almost 50.

One of the oldest guys, Dave, liked to have an afternoon nap shortly after lunch. But this was work so how could he do it?

Well, quite easily. He would sit at his desk, laying his head in his left hand, and a pencil in his right hand. Then as he dozed he managed to move his right hand from side to side giving the impression that he was writing training material. And he was never caught by management.

However, his colleagues were not going to allow it to happen without having a little fun. Waiting for him to reach the sleeping zone and then making him awaken abruptly was the order of the day.

From positioning a rotary dial telephone (with its ring volume on the loudest setting) next to him and then making a call to it, or standing behind him and mimicking the manager shouting 'Blakeney!' always resulted in Dave almost falling out of his seat in shock.

Not having wireless systems in those days meant that if you wanted to talk to someone who wasn't at their desk, you would ring the girl on the switchboard and ask her to put out a tannoy announcement to ask the person you wanted, to ring you on your extension.

One day, a chap called Roy rang Barbara, the switchboard girl and told her to tannoy "Ted Rogers to

THE SKY'S THE LIMIT
Techology leads the way at GEC Plessey Telecommunications (GPT). Above, an aerial view of Edge Lane in the 1960s (picture courtesy of Julian Taylor)

Some of the Plessey staff who worked at Edge Lane for many years

ring 321" – remember Dusty Bin? – which she duly did. Well almost. She announced: "Attention please, will Ted Rogers please ring 32... bloody hell!"

Seconds later the head of personnel came bouncing down two flights of stairs and stormed into our office area where he was joined by our manager demanding to know which of us 'bloody idiots' had requested the announcement.

Needless to say that none of us could answer even if we wanted to, because we couldn't stop laughing.

One spring day, in the mid 1990s, I was walking across the Marconi site through the landscaped gardens towards the covered way.

It was a beautiful sunny day and I bumped into a lot of people.

So many, in fact, that I remember thinking to myself, 'this is an amazing place'. I could probably walk around the whole site and speak to maybe a thousand or more people.

People who I knew the names of, or who I recognised as a familiar face. People who I didn't necessarily know exactly what they did in the company, but nonetheless people who I felt I

Just starting out at GEC Plessey Telecommunications

knew personally or could say 'hello' to.

They in turn could probably do the same to scores or hundreds or perhaps even more of the other employees on the site.

And although we were all here because we were employed and paid by a multi-national telecommunications firm, we were all here, I thought, in our own community. Our very own small town. And this was perhaps 20 years after I had first started work at the site, which had then

employed maybe two to three times more people than it did at that time. The site was much more than a place of work. It was a community of people who were very much connected to each other.

It was a significant part of the culture and heritage of the city of Liverpool. Perhaps far more than those who didn't work there will ever know.

To share your memories of life at AT&E, Plessey, GPT or Marconi, visit www.plesseyattheedge.co.uk

The Work Study Dept at Plessey in 1979
(picture courtesy of Colin Roberts)

In 1972, workers at Plessey started a fund to support a co-worker who had been diagnosed with a serious medical problem. The fund grew into a registered charity, Save a Life, which raised hundreds of thousands of pounds from Plessey, GPT and Marconi employees at Edge Lane. This photograph shows staff from GPT Edge Lane in 1993, presenting equipment for detecting sight problems to St Paul's Eye Unit at the Royal Hospital

Plessey staff remembered in this photo from Linda McGee

Harold Wilson during a visit to Plessey in 1977, with Ken Lilley, managing director at Edge Lane

WINNING TEAM

Staff from the Marketing Communications department at the Marconi Challenge in 1999

STREETLIFE

UPS AND DOWNS

Joe Cooney spent much of his working day clinging, spiderlike, to a wire suspended from a 90ft crane in Old Hall Street. His job – to secure the hawser sections of the 20ft columns on the old Cotton Exchange. In 1967 the columns were being carefully removed, so to see them safely down, Joe made the 75ft trip with each section

Cazneau Street fruit market in the 1940s

Touching up the paintwork 240 feet up, at the top of the Municipal Buildings, 1959

A delivery of casks of rum, arriving for storage in Speke at the House of Seagram

A scrap car is removed by workers in 1966

A CLEAN SWEEP

Corporation workmen demonstrate new automatic street cleaners at St John's Precinct in 1971. The new vaccuum-type cleaners looked rather odd. So wouldn't the sweepers feel rather embarrassed walking around the city pushing them? Gerry Parsley, a traditional sweeper for four years and part of the new automated brigade, said: "I never felt embarrassed pushing round the old cart, so I am hardly likely to feel embarrassed now."

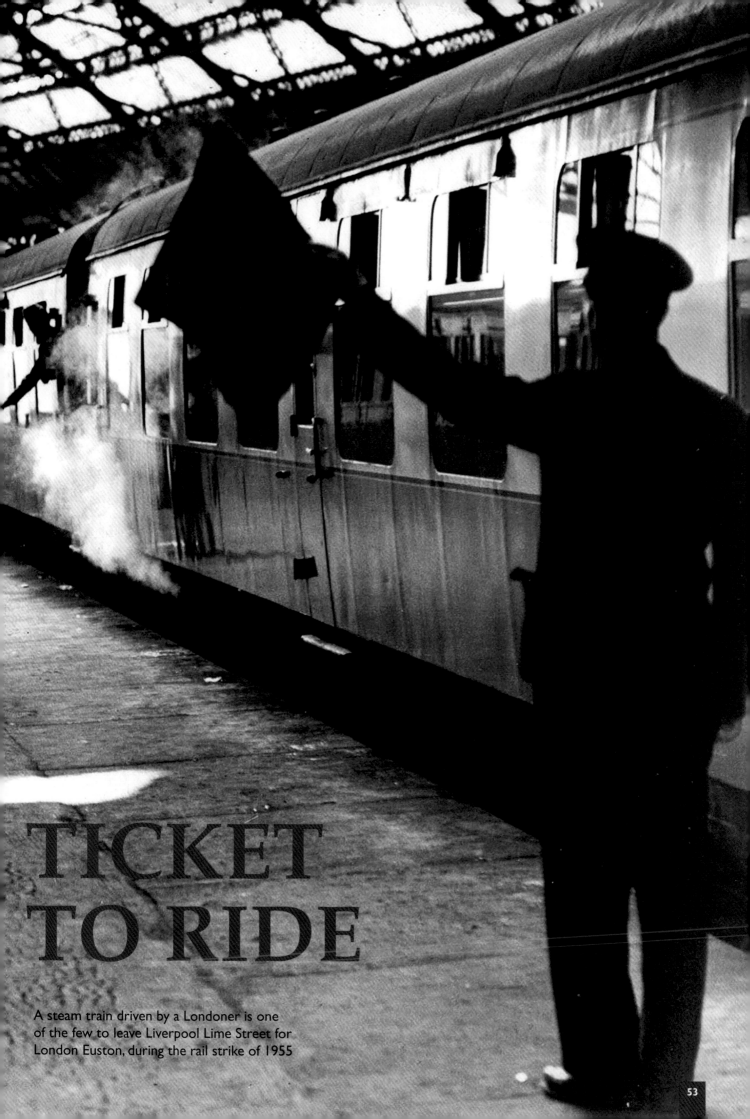

TICKET
TO RIDE

A steam train driven by a Londoner is one
of the few to leave Liverpool Lime Street for
London Euston, during the rail strike of 1955

END OF THE LINE

The last train departed from Liverpool's Exchange Station in April 1977. Driver Bill Potter signs autographs in his cab for Steven Stanley and Graeme Orr in Lime Street Station. Below left, the green flag is waved for the last time at Exchange Station in April 1977 – Jack Hesketh of Formby records the train leaving the station

Operating the new £1m railway control room at Skelhorne Street, Liverpool, in 1946

ONE WAY TICKET

Ticket collectors Bill Barber (left) and Tommy Roberts, ponder the demolition of Liverpool Central Station in 1971

CHOCS AWAY

Above, transporting Cadbury's goods across the railway network, and left, animal feed is loaded onto the train, 1961

In 1956, workmen unearthed the original tracks on which George Stephenson's Rocket ran its inaugural trip from Crown Street, Liverpool, to Manchester, in 1830, thus beginning the world's first inter-city rail service. Unhappily, William Huskisson, MP for Liverpool, was run over on the maiden trip, becoming the first rail fatality. However, the expressions on the faces of these men, do not suggest history in the making...

JOSEPH BLAKE,
146 & 154, MOUNT PLEASANT
COACH BUILDER

Carriage-making firm Blake's of Mount Pleasant. This picture, taken at the end of the 1800s, shows, seated, James Graham Reece (left) and his father-in-law Joseph Blake (right)

PLEASED AS PUNCH

The ladies of the cash ticket and punch department do what it says on the door sign and prepare the tickets and punch machines for Liverpool Corporation's trams and buses. This picture was taken circa 1930s, in the tramways head office, probably in Hatton Garden

THIRSTY WORK

Left, the cleaning and servicing bay at Stanley Bus Park, where workmen can be seen shampooing one of the buses, 1965. Below, Vivien Munns and Mary Brown serve refreshments to passengers during a flight from Liverpool Airport in 1968

The end of the clippies was heralded by this bold experiment by Liverpool Corporation in July, 1956, to introduce the first one-man bus

ON THE
BEAT

NEW RECRUITS
Left, Liverpool's first women police officers – Inspector Bushell and Sergeant Ashmore – being sworn in by Councillor Bailey, chairman of the Liverpool Watch Committee, in 1947

ON THE BALL
Liverpool and Bootle Police cadets squad get in training at Mather Avenue for the National Police Cadets Football Cup in 1973

LOST & FOUND
It happens every day – a policewoman on duty at Princes Landing Stage takes a lost toddler to the nearby Police Station, 1968

MINI ADVENTURE
Presumably not part of undercover operations, the launch of an anti-crime Christmas campaign in the 1970s, outside police headquarters on Hope Street

DRIVING AMBITION

Above, police drivers get set to take the advanced driving test in 1967

ON THE CASE

You have the right to remain silent...every day life isn't all blues and twos for these police officers, catching up on the local news in 1947

Liverpool City Police line-up for the semi-final of the National Police Cup in 1960

SPECIAL BRANCH

A warm welcome for new specials, as 30 new recruits are inducted into the Merseyside Special Constabulary at Hardman Street police headquarters in 1974

Envelopes being alphabetically sorted at the Unity Football Pools headquarters in Liverpool, in 1940. Unity Pools operated throughout the Second World War. It was formed, at the Government's behest, from the three major pools companies: Littlewoods, Zetters and Vernons

LUCKY NUMBERS

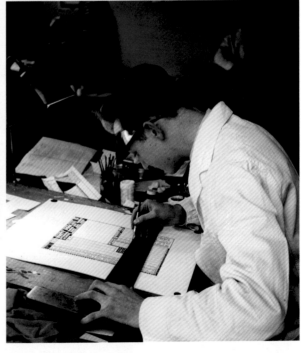

X MARKS THE SPOT

A general view of one of the four large pool rooms at Littlewoods in 1949, where the women check coupons against the weekends results

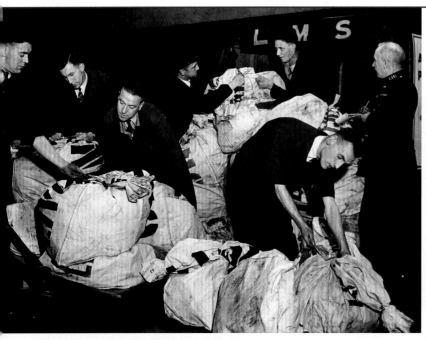

SIGNED, SEALED, DELIVERED

Mail bags being received and checked in at the
headquarters of Unity Football Pools in Liverpool, in 1939

ICON OF THE CITY

The iconic Littlewoods building on Edge Lane, pictured in 1989. Top right, hoping for a bright future in
1983, Pat Thomas with staff outside the Littlewoods JM Centre at Old Hall Street

STAND AND DELIVER

LABELLED WITH LOVE

Top, counter clerks at Liverpool's Victoria Street Post Office have the ladies in giggles. Above, the General Post Office in Victoria Street in 1941 and left, the telegraph room, pictured around the turn of the century

Above, Victoria Street GPO in December 1964. Below, sorting through the Christmas post

POLE POSITION
Edward Wardle seems to draw the short straw as the apprentice in 1968, while the rest of the team, David Ellis, Brian Evans and Philip Harris, check on the ground work

Down-to-earth work for apprentice Stewart Reid as he checks the wiring of circuits at the Post Office training centre in 1968, with the help of David Smethen

THE POWER AND THE MONEY

BOOM TOWN

The scene in the Liverpool Fruit Exchange in April 1969, with the auctioneer conducting the business. Right, the Water Department's operations room at the Municipal Buildings on Dale Street, 1963. Opposite page, Martins Bank pictured in 1964

Members bidding in the ring at the Cotton Exchange in the late 1950s

COTTON ON

Right, Lord Woolton addresses grandees and staff at the reopening by the Earl of Derby of the Liverpool Cotton Exchange and Futures Market in the great hall on Old Hall Street, in May 1954, after government control from 1941. Although still with us, rebuilding in 1967 changed the Cotton Exchange beyond recognition

RINGING OUT

Before mobile phones...the announcement of the members' 'warning bell' by Sergeant Ridings in the Cotton Exchange in 1954. Below, a scene during the bidding of wheat for the Liverpool Wheat Futures Market, at Wellington Buildings, 1953

BURNING AMBITION

BY ROYAL APPOINTMENT

It was Edna Carribine's golden moment in 1983, when she was chosen to present a bouquet of flowers to Princess Margaret during her visit to the Bryant & May factory. Edna's date with royalty was arranged to mark her 43 years of unbroken service in the boxmaking department of the Speke firm. Below, the Bryant & May factory in 1979

BAT workers made redundant are 'piped out' by a line piper at the Commercial Road factory in 1984

Elsie O'Neil and friends in the Ogden's snuff mill in 1989

Happy 'Higsonians' – the driving force of Higson's Brewery. Opposite page, a delivery to The Nook in Chinatown, and huge bags of hops piled high in Higson's hop store

I'LL DRINK TO THAT!

Brewing is their business and these members of the Higson's team salute the brewery in 1982 – pictured left to right are Chris Hellin, Stewart Thompson, Gordon Barrack, Peter Donegan, Paul Bauer and Harry Bell

SWEET TASTE OF SUCCESS

LICENSED TO CHILL

Above, Pendleton's workers
Paul Lonergan and Mary
Bradley make a clean sweep
for success in 1993. Right,
stop me and try one – the
ice vendors' trike in 1970

ICE ICE BABY

Left, Lynda Priest celebrates being in the lolly with a bingo win from Kirkby's Gala Club in 1993 – but Lynda had another reason to celebrate, as the Kirkby ice cream plant was back in action thanks to workers who refused to give up hope after their sacking by Clarke Foods. In April, they were back at work and rushing to complete their first order. Former Lyons Maid employees gave up their weekend to work at the former Lyons Maid factory. Below, ice lollies, choc ices and cones are sampled by Pendleton's staff in 1976

They've got it licked – Wally Smith and staff at Pendletons Ice Cream, Kirkby, 1993

FROZEN ASSETS

Calogiro and Vincenzo Mancuso at their ice cream factory in Tuebrook, in 1978. In 1951, Calogiro said 'arrivederci' to his family in Sicily and set out in search of fame and fortune in Liverpool. He set up in a small shop in Lodge Lane, and four years later he was joined by his younger brother Vincenzo. Between them they built up a thriving small business, Mancuso Brothers, ice cream salesmen. Their breakthrough came with motor-driven vans selling soft ice cream, as many will remember. Right, as Britain sizzled in the summer of 1977, Albert Critchley, of the famous family firm, was up at 4.30am to make 30 gallons of ice cream to sell around the Wavertree area

Tate & Lyle workers fighting to keep their jobs, lost the battle in January 1981 – it marked the end of a bitter campaign to keep the company in the city, where in 1859, Henry Tate first began to produce brown sugar from imported canes at his grocery shop in Manesty Lane

FAIRRIE & C°. BRANCH OF TATE & LYLE LTD

SUGAR REFINERS

MUNCH BUNCH

Winners of a competition invited to Sayers' Norris Green bakery to see production of strawberry tarts in 1988 – Vera Boyer, Eileen Barr, Lily Summersgill, Enid Leigh and Mary Ditchfields, with bakery staff Pat Leddon and Joanne Horsley

CRUMBS OF COMFORT

Right, Archbishop Derek Worlock and Anglican Bishop David Sheppard visited the United Biscuits' Crawfords, when it was threatened with closure in 1983

Sealed with love – food parcels being sent out to British forces in the Gulf in 1991, by staff at Jacobs in Aintree

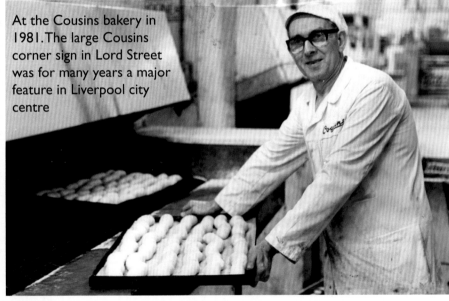

At the Cousins bakery in 1981. The large Cousins corner sign in Lord Street was for many years a major feature in Liverpool city centre

RISING TO THE CHALLENGE

Bill Hornibrook wasn't impressed by the findings of the time and motion experts in 1974. He decided he would go at his own speed. His job as a dough-cutter, at the Davison Frozen Dough factory at Skelmersdale, involved slicing up quarter-ton batches into 9lb units and then feeding them into a machine. The experts reckoned that in a seven-hour shift it was just about possible to deal with 24 batches. But Bill chose to ignore them and do the impossible, managing 30 batches every shift. Bill, who helped produce 100,000 loaves a week, shrugged it all of: "I'm an energetic chap and I work at my own speed. The secret is to get into a rhythm."

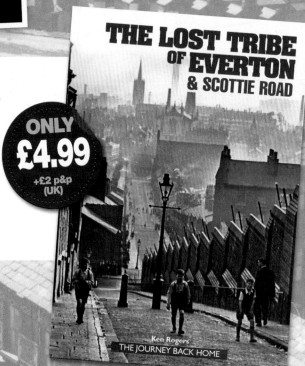

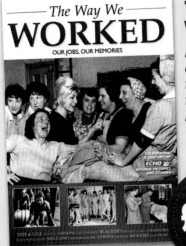
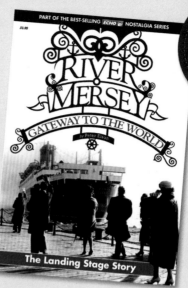

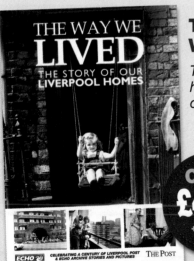

The blacksmith at the
old Edge Lane bus and
tram depot works in
September, 1979